www.tredition.de

AF204200

Dr. Anna Rostomyan born in 1985 is an Assistant Professor of English, Communications Consultant, Researcher, Author, Coach and Reviewer at Sage Publishing, as well as Editorial Board Member at "Academic Star Publishing Company". Her PhD work, which she defended back in 2013 in tight collaboration with the University of Fribourg, Switzerland, Department of Philosophy and Interfaculty Institute for Central and Eastern Europe, being awarded an ASCN PhD research grant, and Yerevan State University, English Philology Department and Chair of English for Cross-cultural communication, was devoted to the linguo-cognitive, pragmatic, neurolinguistic, sociolinguistic and psycholinguistic analysis of the verbal and non-verbal expressions of emotions in English fiction and films.

While interested in a whole range of disciplines as Affective Pragmatics, Psycholinguistics, Sociolinguistics, Neurolinguistics, Cognitive Linguistics, Communication Studies, and Discourse Analysis, her current research and studies are mainly focused on Emotional Intelligence, Neuroeconomics, Neuroleadership, Personal Branding, Emotional Marketing, Business Communication Management, etc.

Apart from academia, she also worked with successful communication and recruitment strategies for such companies as "Porsche Center Yerevan", "ArmenOil", and "Armeconombank" OJSC.

This book is a series of her previous book on business communication management and is particularly meant for the Business world professionals and leaders.

Author contact: annarostom@yahoo.com

Dr. Anna Rostomyan

Your guide to becoming a successful leader

Book description: Leadership is a skill few master. The present book gives you a detailed analysis on the essence and nature of leadership and proposes diverse management strategies and communication techniques, which will eventually enhance your leadership skills. The author speaks about the current developments of Neuroleadership and New Leadership. She also highlights the importance of emotional intelligence in leading people.

www.tredition.de

Verlag und Druck:
tredition GmbH, Halenreie 40-44, 22359 Hamburg

ISBN
Paperback: 978-3-347-21225-1
Hardcover: 978-3-347-21226-8
e-Book: 978-3-347-21227-5

CONTENT

Preface

Since the early ages people have been concerned with the problem of leadership and what is needed to become a good leader.

Many outstanding philosophers dedicated their surveys and public speeches on the issue of successfully leading people, since it is one of the greatest challenges, and, we can also say, gift of all.

Leadership is, in essence, the art of motivating a group of people to act toward achieving a certain common goal. In a business setting, this can mean directing workers and colleagues with a specific strategy to meet the company's needs.

Leadership particularly captures the essentials of being able and prepared to inspire others: and here inspiration includes both yourself and your team members, co-workers and employees.

A leader actually inspires others to act while simultaneously directing the way they act. He or she is an inspiration for everybody around and has to lighten the way, which they pursue.

A leader should, hence, be the guide and the lighthouse, lightening and showing the way to the others.

In the recent years, leadership has a bit changed its former scope; thus, paying much more attention to the people's needs and demands, their desires and longings, feelings and emotions.

The main scope of the leaders has become their human resources, as they are no longer considered to be merely working machines, but the most significant proportion in achieving a certain objective or a specific goal.

Hence, the human factor gains prominence in leading people, which should be the main objective of any leader, who wants to have better results.

Truly, in case leaders pay much more attention to the needs of their people, they will stand a better chance of achieving their goals and inspiring others to become better in whatever road they pursue and whatever they do.

The Essence of Leadership

Leadership is an art and it is a skill to be mastered, which can be done only by the bravest.

It is also a decision to be made, which has to be followed.

Making the **decision** to be a leader is a tough one, but it is also the greatest **freedom** you could ever give yourself in this life, and who doesn't like freedom and to be free in taking decisive steps towards a certain goal for a better future?

Leadership is the gift that opens up so many new doors and **opportunities** for you and also to those who depend on you.

Leadership gives you the opportunity to own any fear, uncertainty and self-doubt, but much more importantly, it gives you the responsibility to remove that very fear from the others.

It takes you real **courage** to overcome your fear of failure, fear of abandoning your comfort zone and of feeling uncomfortable and to decide on taking responsibility for the others involved.

Hence, as a fearless leader you will have fulfilling days, confusing days, overwhelming days and down-right exhilaratingly tough days. But that's what makes true leaders special; they overcome their fear and make the decision to lead and to succeed.

When dealing with people, a leader has to remember the human nature of the latters. This human element is the part that can be magical about being a fearless leader, who dares taking responsibility and the gear in his very own hands. Just imagine walking into a dark room with no light, the leader should be the light. That's being a fearless leader, and fearless leaders lean-in to their people's thoughts, beliefs, desires, feelings and emotions. This also involves multitasking on the human level, taking into consideration a number of different aspects and factors.

To conclude with, becoming a strong and fearless leader is a life-long pursuit, and each day serves as a new lesson and teaching moment preparing us for greater and greater opportunities in life and as you are presented with these new opportunities and faced with daily problems, think of the strength and faith you are building and how much more prepared you will be for the next even bigger step and greater opportunity.

That is one of the blessings of fearless leadership, each challenge and opportunity makes us stronger for the next one, if we embrace it, if we dedicate ourselves to the objective and if we commit ourselves to be a truly courageous, fearless leader to rise up and lead in your family, your community, and, last but not least, at your company. Embrace it. Love it. Challenge yourself. Become better. Stay hungry and focused. Be a leader. Be successful.

The Nature of Leaders

Leadership is truly inspiring, motivating, thrilling and exhilarating, but it is also truly very challenging.

Leading people is not so easy as it might seem from the first time. People might ask themselves, "What is it that he/she does that I can't do?" But they really shouldn't ask that very question. Why? Because it is by no means an easy task to perform: as a leader, you have to develop agile skills to set a vision people can easily follow, develop strong relationships so that people want to follow, and set certain definite goals so they know how to follow.

A leader is someone who understands his or her own importance and ability in leading others towards a certain goal, which means that they have to have a set objective to be achieved and for that very reason we can state that a leader is someone with a dream.

Having a dream, a leader should have the tools to achieve it and, therefore, this book can serve you in becoming a skilled leader.

This truly comes to suggest that the leader has to have a vision and strategy and know how to show the way to the others to achieve the set goal, as a leader is someone who knows the way, goes the way and shows the way according to John. C. Maxwell.

In fact, knowing the way does not make you a leader: a leader should inspire others to become the best version of themselves, to excel in their endeavours and bring prosperity to the company.

Of course, there are also some narcissistic leaders, who do not take advice from their peers and believe always to be true, but a good leader should pay attention to the special needs of his or her surroundings and take feedback responsibly and readily to become a better version of themselves.

It is also noteworthy that there should be a distinction between as boss and a leader:

1) a boss takes advantage of the work of the others,
2) a leader gives advantage and praises the work of the team.

A leader is always very happy with the achievements of the team members and gives credit to them, so that to motivate them to set more difficult goals and to achieve more.

A successful leader is someone who knows the know-how of leading and is ready to share that very knowledge with the others. He or she is ready to communicate about the mischiefs and drawbacks, which hinder the success of the team and is also ready to support in accomplishing the task.

The good news is that leaders are not born, they are trained to become, they are made and as everything else they are made through daily input, hard work, inspiration and training.

We have, thence, conducted a study to learn what the society thinks about the nature of leaders and to the question of whether they are born to be or trained to become.

We have given that question to business people who have an understanding of what a good leader should be.

The results come to prove that the majority think that leaders are made, that one can be trained with the required skills to become a successful leader, as Vince Lombardi, the American football player and coach, was convinced.

We might come to think that they are right as someone may have inborn qualities of a leader, but because of laziness or lack of interest may not succeed in leading people for a certain objective.

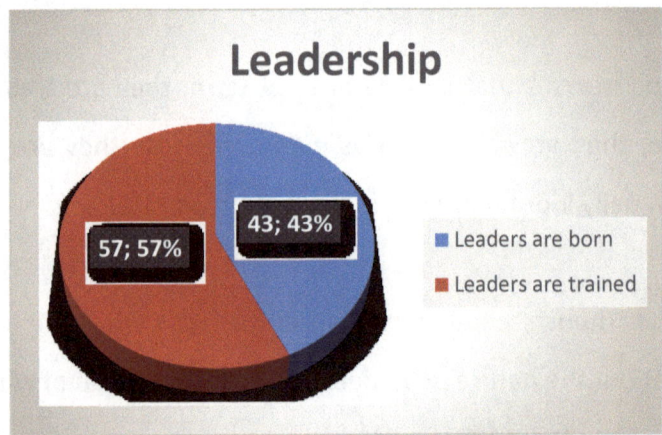

Chart 1: The Types of Leaders

As **Chart 1** shows, the majority are convinced that leaders are generally made through training, hard work, and experience. Though there are also people, who think that leaders are born with inborn qualities of successfully leading people, which can also be considered as true, since inborn qualities + hard work make up an unbeatably great leader.

It is also noteworthy that leaders do not become great only by themselves: they become great in bringing their abilities at hand to empower others, to inspire them, to bring the best in others and to guide them accordingly. In fact, this is truly a very challenging process which requires real dedication and experience.

Further, it should be noted that people, as human resources, are really very complex creatures and have their own thoughts, beliefs, desires, dreams, motivations, feelings and emotions. Hence, it becomes the task of the leader to deal with his very own emotions and the emotions of the others around him, raising their self-management and social competence. This can be achieved by emotional intelligence discussed further.

Leadership and Management

Leading people has always been a trait of only a few endowed with leadership skills, as Alexander the Great, Napoleon Bonaparte, Julius Ceasar, Tigran the Great, Cleopatra, etc.

In ancient times clergymen, statesmen and popes were also leaders, as for instance Cardinal Richelieu in France during the reign of King Louis XIII, who sought to consolidate royal and religious power and strengthen France's international position.

People have always looked up with owe to this kind of leaders.

Leadership and **management**: these two notions are very close to one another, but there is a slight distinction to be born in mind.

In fact, **leadership** is not the same as **management** though very similar and linked to it. Managing is very easy as compared to leadership, as it involves accomplishment of various daily tasks that are pretty straight-forward, i.e. see the task, learn the task, analyze the task, do the task, ready, done.

Today, the term "management" is everywhere we can think of, describing, as the corresponding entry in Merriam-Webster's Dictionary (9 September 2015) suggests, *"the act or art of managing: the conducting or supervising of something (as a business)."* (Engwall, Kipping and Üsdiken, 2016: 8).

Yet, it is noteworthy that **management** is a trendy term and even in English the term itself did not come into more widespread use until after World War II, as suggested in Figure 1.1.

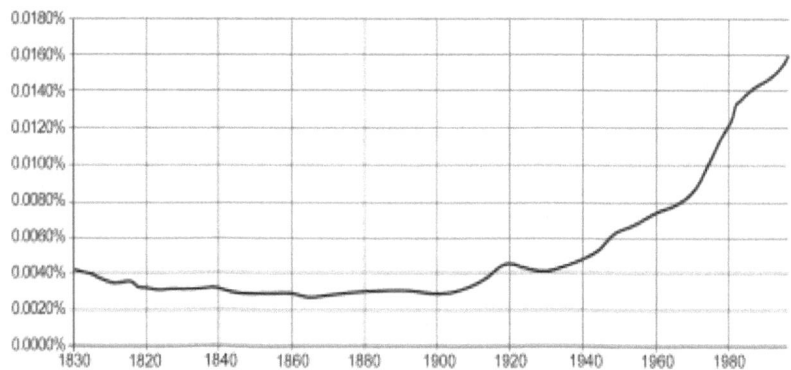

FIGURE 1.1 The Occurrence of "Management" in Google Books 1800–2000

(Figure source: Engwall, Kipping and Üsdiken, 2016: 9)

As we can truly see from the above figure, there has been a drastic rise of the use of the term "management" in the late 20s.

Actually, the terms leadership and management usually tend to be used interchangeably, but they're not at all the same: leadership, as-a-matter-of-factedly, requires traits and characteristic features that extend beyond management duties. Both leaders and managers have to manage the resources at their disposal, but true leadership requires much more than mere management: for example, managers may or may not be described as inspiring by the people working under their supervision, whereas a leader, first and foremost, should inspire those who follow them.

A manager, on the contrary, is someone who directs the co-workers in accomplishing this or that certain task on demand. Although it also includes some leadership skills, this does not include particularly inspiring others to become better.

LEADERSHIP	MANAGEMENT
May or may not be the manager.	May or may not be the leader.
Must inspire followers.	May or may not inspire those under them.
Emphasizes innovation.	Emphasizes rationality and control.
May be unconcerned with preserving existing structures.	Seeks to work within and preserve existing corporate structures.
Typically, operates with relative independence.	Typically, a link in the corporate chain of command.
May be less concerned with interpersonal issues.	May be more concerned with interpersonal issues for peaceful cooperation in the company.
Enjoys working alone.	Enjoys working in a team.
Enjoys more the process.	Enjoys more the results.

Table 1: Leadership vs. Management

(Source: https://www.thebalancesmb.com/leadership-definition-2948275)

As a matter of fact, this opposition can be continued with some overlapping features between leaders and managers. Yet, the most important distinction is that managers may be more likely to preserve existing structures, because they themselves operate within that structure. They may have bosses above them, so they have less freedom to break rules in the pursuit of lofty goals. Leaders, on the other hand, often operate fairly independently. They enjoy the process and enjoy inspiring others. They are role models for the others to depend on and get inspiration from.

Thence, bearing this distinction in mind, we can make a clear-cut difference between leaders and managers.

Besides, it is also noteworthy that managers can have a promotion and be promoted from the position of, for example, a stuff manager to top manager, or else just vice versa, lose their position of a manager and be rotated to a lower position or be fully fired, whereas leaders have a stable stance and being an inspiration to the others always preserve their role.

In fact, in conclusion it should be noted that if a leader has managerial skills and, in reciprocal, a manager has leadership skills, they will consequently flourish in whatever they undertake.

Communication in Leadership

Communication is the keystone in every kind of interaction.

Leaders are generally good communicators, equipped with communication management tools and strategies.

And leaders should by all means communicate well, which ensures better impact and influence on the others, which builds credibility and trust in people towards your persona per se.

Communication is, in fact, a multifaceted process, which involves both of the speaking partners, and for the success of the speech event both of the parties should be open to communication.

We suppose that any leader cannot work at his/her best without proficient communicative skills.

Communication is, in fact, a multi-faceted process and there are different types of communication, namely:

- Verbal communication (written and spoken),
- Non-verbal communication (gestures, gross bodily movements, facial expressions, etc.)
- Visual communication (advertisements, posters, etc.)

(Rostomyan, 2020: 11)

When we think of the ways we use language, we think of face-to-face conversations, telephone conversations, reading and writing, and even talking to oneself. These are arenas of language use - theaters of action in which people do things via language. But what exactly *are* they doing with language? What are their goals and intentions? By what processes do they achieve these goals? In order for one person to understand the other, there must be a kind of "***common ground***" of knowledge between them. This "common ground" from their past conversations, their immediate surroundings, their shared cultural background, as well as their knowledge about their emotions, beliefs, dreams and desires, is of utmost importance in the process of building mutual understanding and peaceful and successful interpersonal interaction. In case there is some kind of mutual understanding between the speakers, this will eventually lead to a drastic reduction of social conflicts (Rostomyan, 2020).

As we know, in order to interpret what is being conveyed in an act of communication, we have to look at various factors, such as: social distance and closeness and, thus, adhere to this or that "*rule of politeness*" not to sound rude, inconsiderate or impolite (Yule, 1996). For instance, to show the social distance between two people an English speaker who considers himself/herself as lower in status, uses forms of address that include a title and a last name, but never the first name unless they are associates or friends (e.g., Mrs. Brown, Dr. Johnson, Pr. Bush, but not John or Steven). This depends greatly on cultural habits which are passed from generation to generation. Thus, we may conclude that each nation has its own *"principles of politeness"*. (Yule, 1996), which also have to be considered in leadership communication.

The above-mentioned examples illustrate the rules in English-speaking communities, whereas in Japanese there are much more forms of addressing, which exactly reflect the distance between the interlocutors. Armenian, which, unlike English, has the "luxury" of singular and plural personal pronouns (դու – Դուք), reflects acts of politeness with the help of grammatical meaning of plurality (Rostomyan, 2013b).

As Verschueren states: "[...] many linguistic choices depend on relationships of *dependence* and *authority*, or *power* and *solidarity*, not only between utterer and interpreter but also between utterer and/or interpreter and any third party which either figures in the topic of the discourse or is otherwise involved." (Verschueren, 1999: 91).

Moreover, for some languages, the concept of *"social relationships"* may be extended to the extent that it can be applied to indicate relationships not only between human beings, but also between people and animals, people and plants, and even people and things. Thus, those very animals, plants and things become an indispensable part of our daily activities. This phenomenon can truly explain the sailor's choice of "she" as the pronoun which is used to refer to a ship, or the choice of a driver to refer to the car by means of the same pronoun in the English language, a language, which normally tends to make all lifeless things grammatically neuter. In fact, it should be kept in mind that all those community-specific communicative roles are strongly culturally-dependent and may vary across cultures. Thus, when being in a new cultural environment one should be able to learn at least the most basic communicative norms so that not to get in a ridiculous or confusing situation (Yule, 1996).

In summary, it should be noted that these norms and principles, emotions and communication are very prominent in leadership, since through successful communication tools leaders can achieve their desired results, as for instance in rhetoric, when the spokesperson uses diverse techniques to influence the audience.

Factually, the analysis of the linguistic mechanisms of verbaliza-tion of emotions in the process of interpersonal communication, which has become quite urgent today, should be realized on the basis of cognitive evaluation of emotivity. The positive and nega-tive emotional predisposition between the interlocutors and their common ground also plays a vital role in the process of decoding any piece of information. It should become the duty of each and every leader to strive towards communicating his/her demands openly and overtly, as the outcome of the project very much de-pends on the communication between the speaking partners, which will consequently help us to create a healthier working at-mosphere and stimulate the successful achievement of a com-mon goal or a certain set objective.

Emotions and Leadership

When leading people, we have to bear in our minds that we are dealing with creatures of emotion, who are usually governed by their previous emotional experiences and mostly rely on their gut instincts.

Here, the concept of **Emotional Intelligence** (EQ) comes to the fore, which is more important in handling relationships than IQ.

Emotional Intelligence mainly includes:

1. *Self- awareness*:
   knowing your inner part,
2. *Self-management*:
   controlling and managing your behaviour,
3. *Social competence*:
   tuning into other people (empathy),
4. *Relationship management*:
   dedicating time and energy into relationships (Goleman, 1995).

Daniel Goleman (1995) speaks a lot about the importance of emotional intelligence in our lives. He describes it as the keystone in dealing with people in different life and workplace situations.

The good news is that this competence can also be learnt through training, practice and emotion management techniques, which are very important for the formation and management of peaceful communicative relations (Rostomyan, 2020).

In fact, as Dale Carnegie (1982) truly states, when dealing with people, we have to keep in mind that we are mostly dealing with people of emotion, and not with people of reason.

This brings us to the assumption that especially when leading people, we have to bear in mind their emotions and feelings, their emotional predisposition towards us, which will greatly contribute to the heightening of social competence and relationship management, which will in its turn enhance our leadership skills and will guide us in successful leading to the desired goal.

Eleanor Roosevelt also mentioned and highlighted the role of our heart, the importance of managing and leading with the heart, stating that when handling others we should be guided by our heart, as only in that case we can know the importance of the others feelings and emotions.

Indeed, recently there has really been much debate on to what extent emotions are rational or whether they are rational or not. Actually, the emotional/rational dichotomy approximates the folk distinction between the human *"heart"* and *"head"*. Sometimes people are sure that something is wrong "in their heads", but "their hearts" tell them just the opposite, or just vice versa: you know something is the right thing to do "in your heart", but "your head" tells you not to.

There is a steady gradient in the ration of rational-to-emotional control over the mind; the more intense the feeling, the more dominant the emotional mind becomes – and the more ineffectual the rational (Goleman, 1995: 9).

Indeed, in those very moments your heart may tell you one thing, whereas your brain – quite another thing: you can, hence, write down the opposite pole thoughts to be able to understand your emotions and give an emotionally rational answer to the situation (Bradberry & Greaves, 2016: 86).

In the heated emotional moment, undergoing very strong uncontrollable emotions, you might be greatly influenced by your strongly felt emotions and might not take the righteous decision to be made. Therefore, it is highly advised to calm down, to count at least to four, and only then to respond to the present outward situation at hand.

Anna Rostomyan (2020) speaks about the importance of the harmonious interrelation of our head and heart, i.e. our emotional and rational minds, as only by means of paying attention to the signals received from both of the aforementioned agents one can have a clear-cut perception of the outward reality.

We do firmly believe that for the successful choice productions of the higher cognitive processes, the emotional and rational minds should work at their best by means of cooperating with one another and passing forward important information from the perceived outward stimuli (Paronyan & Rostomyan, 2011a; Rostomyan, 2013b).

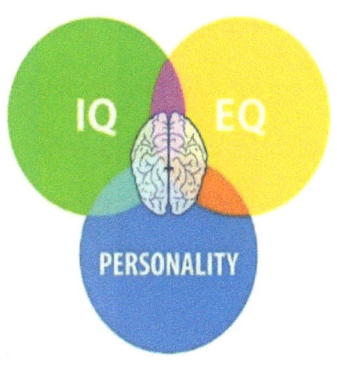

Chart 2: The EQ & IQ Dichotomy[1]
(Chart source: Rostomyan, 2020: 72)

In tune with modern theorists of emotions (cf. Ortony, Clore, Collins, LeDoux, et alias), we regard emotions essentially as subconscious signals and evaluations that inform, modify and receive feedback from higher cognitive processes. In a sense, we have to admit that human beings have two minds, which are closely interrelated **– *emotional*** and ***rational***.

In essence, these two minds, the emotional (EQ) and the rational (IQ), generally operate in firm harmony, intertwining their very

1 Chart graphic design by Sona Safaryan, MA in Arts.

different ways of knowing to guide us through the world. Ordinarily, there is a balance between the emotional and rational minds, with emotion feeding into and informing the operations of the rational mind, and the rational mind refining and sometimes vetoing the inputs of the emotions. Yet, these two minds, the emotional and the rational one, are semi-dependent faculties, each reflecting the operation of distinct, but interconnected circuitry in the brain, which together have an influence on our personality (Paronyan, Rostomyan, 2011b; Rostomyan, 2012, Rostomyan & Rostomyan, 2018).

As we see, information from both of the agents EQ & IQ is important for the efficient functioning of the brain in evaluating and understanding the perceived stimuli and outward situation.

Thence, both the emotional intelligence (EQ) and rational quotient (IQ) are crucial in leadership, especially in neuroleadership, which will be thoroughly discussed later.

It is true that in the heated emotional moment rationality does not perform at its best, but only adhering to pure dry facts may leave out a great deal of important information, which can also bring facts to the overall interpretation of the received data.

Therefore, we do firmly believe that the harmonious interaction of the two can drastically help us in handling life situations and correspondingly respond to them.

Indeed, if we only rely purely on dry facts, we can miss a great deal of important information, and just vice versa, if we focus only on emotional information, we might miss the facts.

The interrelation between emotion and cognition can be seen in **Chart 2** presented below:

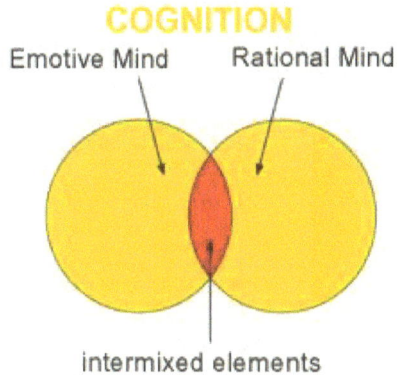

Chart 3: The Interrelation of Emotional and Rational Minds altogether shaping human Cognition[2]

(Chart source: Rostomyan, 2015: 1275)

---

[2] Chart graphic design by Arman Sargsyan, BA in Arts and Design.

According to Daniel Goleman, if the emotional mind follows the logic and its rules, with one element standing for another and co-operating with one another, things need not necessarily be defined by their objective identity; what matters is how they are perceived; things are as they seem. What something reminds us of can be far more important that what it "is" (Goleman, 1995: 338). Hence, the balanced collaboration of the aforementioned two *"human minds"* is very essential in interpersonal communication in every sphere of activity: actually, these two minds continuously cooperating with each other endorsing or vetoing certain emotions and their communicative expressions (Paronyan, Rostomyan, 2011a: 26-33).

Nowadays, as we have already given stated, very often scientists speak about Emotional Intelligence (EQ) as compared with purely Rational Intelligence (IQ), and which is more striking, preference is given to the former one as this mainly contributes to the creation of peaceful relations.

Daniel Goleman identified the five *"domains"* of EQ as:

1. *Knowing* your emotions.
2. *Managing* your own emotions.
3. *Motivating* yourself.

4. *Recognizing* and understanding other people's emotions.

5. *Managing* relationships, i.e., managing the emotions of others (Goleman, 1995).

Yet, it is also noteworthy that under certain circumstances the balance between cognitive and emotive minds gets lost: emotions come to prevail and, as a result, one loses the ability to properly estimate the situation at hand. Truly, in the heat of emotional obsession the ability to regulate his/her thoughts, behaviour and speech can be extremely diminished, and in these situations, one should take pains not to let emotions govern the rational part of the brain: once we lose the balance, we are sure to make wrong decisions and wrongly evaluate diverse situations. Consequently, we may even misinterpret different messages from the external world and respond to them inappropriately. This is the reason why when we are emotionally upset or anxious about something, we often state that we *just can't think straight*. The fact of being emotionally distressed can even hinder one's ability to learn and work properly and effectively.

Sometimes, the influence of the emotions (positive or negative) is so enormous that the emotional mind becomes prevailing and one does not manage to control it and, as a result, our strongly felt emotions are being consequently manifested on the outside.

Hence, this fact actually finds its verbal and/or non-verbal manifestation – we say things for which we may later regret. Consequently, it is advisable that the emotional-rational balance should be kept in order not to be exposed to bewildering and misleading situations and subsequent misinterpretations. A good and sensible piece of advice which, unfortunately, is often so difficult for many of us to follow (Rostomyan, 2013b; Rostomyan, 2020).

Hence, it follows from the above that we should also admit that cognitive purely rational intelligence cannot work at its best potential without emotional intelligence. Therefore, to learn the objectivity of the outward reality, we should rely on the information perceived from both head and heart; thence, their harmonoius cooperation is vitally essential for us, especially for the leaders, who have responsibility for the others.

Neuroleadership and New Leadership

If we look at the evolution of **leadership**, we can pinpoint that nowadays we have reached a state, where we need to under- stand everything on the 'neuro' level, including leadership.

Neuroscience is a multidisciplinary science that is concerned with the study of the structure and function of the nervous system.

Neuroleadership refers to the application of the findings from neuroscience to the field of leadership.

As the leader is a human being, who is not devoid of neurons and emotions, thence, a newly coined term is nowadays used, which is **Neuroleadership** that deals with the emotions of the people in the process of leadership, which we have already given stated in our previous discussions.

The rise of neuroleadership in the workplace and in leadership is elevating organizational behavior practice and theory to a new standard worthy of thorough consideration.

This term was first coined by David Rock, CEO of Results Coaching Systems, in the US publication Strategy+Business in 2006 (Lafferty & Alford, 2010).

It grew out of a need to understand more about how we could be better and more successful leaders, to be more effective at leading and guiding others and ourselves by means of engaging with what our brain and heart tell us about the nature and desires of the being human.

The term *"Neuroleadership"* comes to suggest that for being able to lead we have to control the neuropsychological level of all the interactants involved, that is to say that leaders should be aware of both their feelings and emotions and those of their protégés and collaborators.

Neuroleadership brings neuroscientific knowledge into the areas *of leadership development, management training, change management, education, consulting* and *coaching*.

What makes neuroleadership so innovative is that it provides solutions for professionals based on the human nature, taking into account the emotions and feelings, beliefs and desires both of the leader and everyone else involved.

There are various activities and skills that the leader should be equipped with on the neuro level. These are:

a) Decision making and problem-solving,

b) Emotional regulation,

c) Emotional intelligence (EQ),

d) Social inclusion,

e) Influencing others,

f) Inspiring others,

g) Leading others.

All this comes to prove that emotional intelligence, including (a) self-awareness, (b) self-management, (c) social competence, (d) relationship management (Goleman, 1995) is of great significance, which has to be fully mastered.

As for decisions, according to the philosopher Plato, men take decisions far more following their hearts, and not their reason, even in such a fact-driven field as Economics (Rostomyan, 2015).

We have conducted a survey among economists at a big banking corporation wanting to find out what they think about the role of emotions in business and wanting to find out whether while taking decisions they are influenced by their emotions or not. The results come to prove that they are aware of the role of the emotions and their importance at workplace, yet they take decisions more according to the rational thinking, rather than by reason. Nonetheless, it is noteworthy that though the majority claim that they take decisions following their reason, there are people, who have answered that emotions also influence decision making processes.

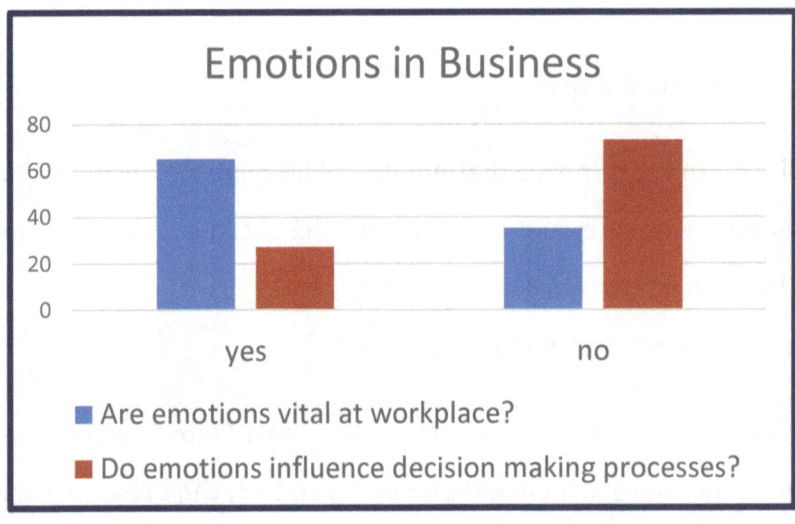

Diagram 1: The role of emotions in business

The diagram comes to proves that workforces are well-aware of the importance of emotions in business, yet they should have a guide, the leader, who would take care of their emotional well-being and emotional safety.

Moreover, to better understand the concept of Neuroleadership, we have to understand the psychological nature of the leader, which will be discussed in this chapter, and here decision-making processes are of paramount importance.

R. Frager and J. Fadiman (2006) explain that according to William James, the founder of Neuropsychology, there are at least five different kinds and layers of our own self, which are very essential when dealing with people, since we cannot lead our teams, in case we are not well aware of our inner crafts, as well as strong and weak sides. Therefore, the five-folded depiction of our "self" is briefly presented below:

Our "Self": this is the inner feeling of our being every morning we wake up. All the psychological processes are rooted in this perspective of the "neuro-self". This layer of the "self" is discreetly and continuously and incessantly present in all the other layers of our "I" (Knowles & Sibicky 1990).

The Biological "Self": this is our biological, physical being which is embodied in our heritage of our ancestors, our DNA. The construction, outer figure of our "self" and all the interrelated psychological processes form our biological "self". This unique "ship" carries us till we pass away from this real world. This is our exceptional heart, our outstanding brain, our brilliant hands, our feet, our tongues, i.e. the physiological aspect of our individuality which makes us different from one another. Our biological "I" can be viewed as the multiple composition of our real "I".

The Real (Material) "Self": this is the layer which encompasses all the object which the individual identifies as composites of his/her own self, such as *mother, father, sister, brother, husband, wife, children, grandparents, relatives, friends*, etc. This means that the house you live in, your family and friends all they emerge into your "real self". The more a person identifies another person as identical with him/her, the better they become part of his/her "self".

The Social "Self": we happily or indulgently or not so happily get involved in the roles that life and fortune gift us. One and the same person can have a number of different roles; thus, having diverse social "selves". These "selves" may be consistent or may change and be variable depending on the situational context. According to W. James to act appropriately means to find the according social "self", which corresponds to the needs of the aroused situation **(Frager & Fadiman 2006: 21-26).**

The Spiritual "Self": this is the subjective inner essence of the personality. This element is co-existent and prevalent in all other layers of our "selves". William James very much wanted to find out why we consider ourselves as something prior to the sum of all the other existing things surrounding us; thus, as a result of his investigations he found out that it is some kind of "spiritual power". William James was not fully assured of the definite existence of the "soul" of human beings, but he supposed that the *individual identification* is not all. He explained from his own experience that there as a constant continuum of cosmic consciousness from which our individuality is separated by inconsistent layers where our other selves are kept as a boundless see or reservoir (Murphy & Ballou 1960: 324).

When speaking about the *"spiritual self"*, we should like to mention that Pope Francis has declared the Armenian monk St. Gregory of Narek, century mystic, theologian and poet, revered in particular by Armenian Catholics, a doctor of the church. Saint Gregory of Narek is a saint of the Armenian Apostolic Church and wrote a book of lamentations called "Narek", which is considered to have spiritual and psychological healing power.

Saint Gregory of Narek

Author of "*Narek*" –
Book of prayers

Picture source: https://en.wikipe-dia.org/wiki/Gregory_of_Narek

This book of prayers is a speech from the depth of the author's heart asking for forgiveness and healing from God.

Hence, being well-aware of the psychological human nature of both the leader himself/herself and those who are led, will greatly contribute to the realization of the project at hand.

Neuroleadership is actually the study of leadership through the lens of neuroscience and explores central elements of leadership, including: (a) *self-awareness* (b) self-management, (c) *awareness of others*, (d) *insight*, (e) *decision making*, and (f) *influencing*.

These qualities play a great role in shaping a good leader, and in its turn, help the latter build a successful team.

As a new field of study, neuroleadership brings neuroscientific knowledge into the area of leadership development, management training, education, consulting and coaching. Neuroleadership largely makes use of Emotional Intelligence which is the ability to assess, identify and control emotions, both in ourselves and in other people (Rostomyan & Sukiasyan, 2015).

In fact, we are all always experiencing some sort of emotion or feeling. Our emotional state varies along the day depending on what happens to us and on the stimuli that we perceive. However, we may not always be conscious of it; that is to say, we may not know or express with clarity which emotion we are experiencing in a given moment. The experience and expression of emotions comprise a routine, yet extraordinarily complex and influential facet of the human experience, particularly in the realm of interpersonal interaction (Rostomyan, 2012).

Therefore, emotional intelligence (EQ) gains its proper significance when interacting with others, especially in achieving of a certain goal, which includes involving in a variety of activities.

The following picture illustrates the actions leading to a high level of Emotional Intelligence.

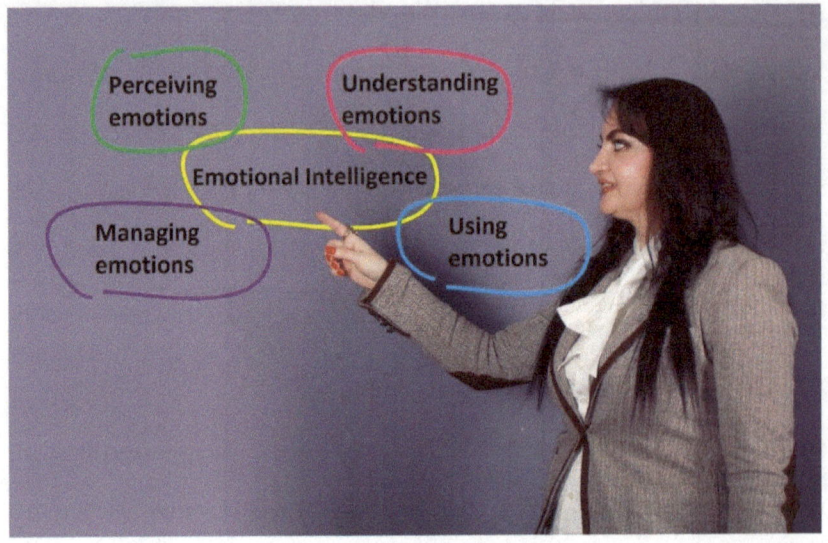

Picture by Arman Sargsyan©

As illustrated in the picture above, emotional intelligence (EQ) involves various activities, such as:

a) perceiving emotions,

b) understanding emotions,

c) using emotions, and

d) managing emotions (Goleman, 1995).

As for New Leadership, in these times of digitalization, the main focus of leadership has been displaced from the goal to the person, to the human factor. Here, the leader and his/her team gain significance, and the emotions and feelings of this or that person involved becomes the keystone in achieving milestones.

The present situation of remote work and New Work, displaces the former concepts of hierarchy and a flatter and flattened workplace relations come to replace it. Here again, the main focus is on the human being completing this or that task, who is a creature endowed with emotions, which is a very clever footstep, as far more of what can be achieved depends on the doer, who will perform better in case of feeling more appreciated on the emotional level.

To sum up with, Neuroleadership and New Leadership bring new objectives to life, which greatly cherish the human factor, put an emphasis to it, value the human input and appreciate progress, which eventually undoubtedly leads to better labour output and more drastic positive results.

Emotion Management in Leadership

As we have seen from our earlier discussions, emotions play a very vital role in dealing with people and leading them.

Thence, emotion management comes to the fore, as to be a successful leader, one has to understand his/her own emotions and the emotions of everybody involved, as well as appropriately managing them to ensure peaceful and successful collaboration.

Arlie Hochschild (1983) coined a new term in his book "The Managed Heart", namely the term *"emotional labour"*, which means that people should behave in a certain pattern and manner according to their professions, and leaders are not an exception.

Anna Rostomyan (2013a) speaks about 5 different emotion expression management techniques proposed by Andersen and Guerrero (1998), which will be briefly discussed below:

1. *Intensification* (or *maximization*) refers to creating the appearance that emotions are felt more strongly than they are. It is important to note that intensification involves the display of an emotion that is genuinely felt; its display is simply exaggerated (see Andersen and Guerrero, 1998).

In fact, people sometimes when feeling an emotion express it more strongly than they actually feel it. For instance, if a person is slightly surprised, he/she may act as if the surprise is exceedingly high. Likewise, if someone feels somewhat sad, he/she may express an overwhelming portion of grief. Other examples of intensification include laughing generously at something, which is only slightly amusing, etc. It is also noteworthy that intensification seems to be used both with positive and negative emotions. Via intensification the speaker may basically have an emotive influence on the interlocutors, subtly suggesting to them what emotions they should feel (Rostomyan, 2013b; Rostomyan, 2020).

Let us observe the following example from crime fiction, which is a true stance of intensifying your speech by means of emotive boosters, i.e. intensifiers, such as *very, truly, greatly, fully*, etc.

Example: *"Yes, sir. Mr. Burns is trying to have my client executed. I'd like to keep him from doing that."*

Judge Buford's mouth turned up in half a smile.

*"**Very** well. Overruled."*

(Gimenez, The Colour of Law, 2007: 428)

In the aforementioned extract, the speakers are lawyers, and one of them is the Judge. The first speaker describes the situation, claiming that he is truly inclined towards defending his client for which the Judge is very pleased: on the non-verbal level the Judge uses a smile, which is a transmitter of positive emotions, and on the verbal level he uses the intensifying adverb "very" to show his positive emotions, his positive predisposition towards his interlocutor and his content and satisfaction for the work of his subordinate lawyer. In fact, being a leader, the Judge knows that he should appraise the good work of his co-workers for them to be inspired and motivated to do more and achieve more.

As we have given stated, for this very reason there exist certain function words called intensifiers, which can be used to achieve positive emotive impact on your interlocutor, such as *very, truly, deeply, greatly, unbelievably, marvellously*, etc. (Buzarov, 1998).

Yet, there are also cases of negative emotive emphasis achieved by such intensifiers as *damn(ed), goddamn(ed), goddamnably, darn(ed)*, etc. as illustrated in the following stretch of discourse:

> Example: *Scott laughed now. "Well, sure, Harry, straightening out your golf swing, that's **pretty goddamned** important."* (Gimenez, The Colour of Law, 2007: 459)

What we learn here from the context is that Scott is most probably angry with his interlocutor as instead of doing the job, he is
attracted to golf. To show his negative emotions, Scott uses the
negative intensifying adverb "*goddamned*" to show his discon-
tent. Yet, it should by all means be also noted that the intensifier
"goddamned" is context-dependent as it can also be used in a
positive context as in "*She is **goddamnably** beautiful*". In this
case, the negative semantic meaning of "goddamned" attached
to the positive semantic meaning of the adjective "beautiful" am-
plifies drastically the overall positive emotive meaning by means
of clash of meaning. The other intensifier used in this example is
the intensifying adverb "pretty", which is also context-dependent
as the intensifying adverb "very" and is synonymous to it, as seen
below:

Pretty		Very	
Positive	*Negative*	*Positive*	*Negative*
pretty good	*pretty* bad	*very* good	*very* bad
pretty easy	*pretty* difficult	*very* easy	*very* difficult

Thus, by means of using emotive emphasizing intensifiers in your speech, you stand a better chance of having your desired positive or negative emotive influence on your interactant.

2. De-intensification (or *minimization*) refers to giving the impression that emotions are felt less strongly than they are. However, it should by all means be mentioned that only part of the felt emotion is hidden, while some portion of it is being displayed. As with intensification, de-intensification involves the display of an emotion which is genuinely felt; its display is merely softened. Actually, sometimes people feel an emotion and display it on the outside, without being able to suppress the expression of the felt emotion, yet they express it not as strongly as they feel it. For instance, if a person is angry with someone, he/she may simply exhibit mild irritation rather than revealing all of his/her anger.

There are also some other cases of de-intensification, where by means of hedging the speaker leaves some space for doubt, as shown in the next stretch of discourse:

Example: *"Well, I agree with you. But doesn't this demonstration prove something else, something important about the killer?"*

Agent Hu frowned. "I'm sorry?"

"The killer was right-handed."

Agent Hu's expression revealed his realization. Yes, **most** *likely the killer would have been right-handed."*

(Gimenez, The Colour of Law, 2007: 415-416)

In the given extract, Agent Hu uses a hedging "most" saying "most linkely" most probably to secure him from mistake. In fact, in the language of law and very often in leadership and management, people avoid using exact statements and sometimes adhere to use of hedged and de-intensified suppositions leaving some space for further speculation and doubt.

3. Simulation refers to displaying an emotion which is not genuinely felt. Such efforts seem to be misleading. Buller and Burgoon suggest that here deception is embodied in intentionally encoding a message by a sender to foster a false deduction by the receiver (Buller and Burgoon, 1998: 381-402). However, in contrary to its reputation, deception can be viewed as a behavioural competent in interpersonal relations (Rostomyan, 2020: 102).

Very often leaders simulate their emotions when they have doubt to keep their dependent motivated to achieve the set goal.

In business generally people often adhere to this very emotion expression management technique simulating their emotions to preserve the image of a successful person as shown in the next example:

> Example: *Scott squeezed the knot of his silk tie, smoothed his $2,000 suit, and whispered back through brilliant white teeth, "Henry, you don't get laid or elected telling the truth."* (Gimenez, The Colour of Law, 2007: 428)

In this extract, we see that Scott is perfectly dressed: as they say you have to be dressed appropriately when climbing the career ladder to be accepted accordingly until you are on top. Here, we can also reveal that people very often cling to this emotion expression management technique, falsifying their outward emotion expression, as Scott himself asserts. So do the politicians.

Knapp and Comadena suggest the notion of *'collaborative deception'*, which is recognized by all the parties involved and is being practiced to maintain a presumably shared desire for the smooth flow of interaction and co-operation (Knapp and Comadena 1979: 270-285). One form of the so-called collaborative deception occurs *'when lies are used to mutually benefit the self-esteem of the*

participants' (O'Hair and Cody 1994: 186). Collaborative deception seems especially related to the display rules that foster pre-
dictable social encounters. Simulation, in particular, seems likely
to be used for this purpose, as it is the only management technique, which involves no genuine experience of emotion. The
most frequently cited example of this emotion management technique is smiling when one does not experience such positive emotions as: gladness, happiness, joy, delight, and the like, but for collaborative peaceful interaction displays it (Rostomyan, 2013a:
145; 2013b), or laughing generously at something, which is only
slightly amusing or not amusing at all governed by social cohesion
and social competence.

4. Inhibition involves exposing the appearance of no emotion
when in reality one is feeling a definite sort of emotion. Sometimes people feel an emotion, but do not express it for some reason. Prime examples of inhibition include keeping a straight face
when something seems funny, hiding attraction towards someone, keeping a seemingly calm voice when feeling angry, etc. It
has been proved by diverse linguists and psychologists that people learn to exhibit the expression of certain emotions in due
course of time (Brannigan and Humphries, 1969: 406-408).

The following example describes a situation where one of the interactant is worried about the state of the present affairs, but does not exhibit his worry on the outside and inhibits the experience of his doom and despair.

> Example: *"No, of course not. I'm still Tom Dibrell's lawyer."*
> *Her expression said that she wasn't buying it.*
> *"Rebecca, look. I've got Bobby working the case. He'll get me through it, she'll get convicted, and things will go back to normal. Don't worry."*
> (Gimenez, The Colour of Law, 2007: 128)

Here, Scott is worried as he has been given a very difficult case. Yet, not to cause despair and worry in his wife, he inhibits his felt negative emotions to keep her spirits high, even assuring her that eventually everything will turn out to be all right as Bobby helps him with the given case. In fact, leaders very often adhere to this technique and in case something hinders the achievement of the goal, they remain calm and express calm disposition to assure others that everything is under control and will eventually be great in the end.

5. *Masking* differs drastically from the other management techniques in the way that it involves showing a particular emotion when one is feeling a completely different emotion. For instance, in certain circumstances a person may express happiness, when he/she feels anger. Likewise, someone may show hatred towards another person, when he/she truly loves that person. Masking is believed to be much more difficult to apply than any other emotion management technique *'probably because it is easier to moderate an existing emotion than to express an emotion that is very different from what one is feeling'* (Andersen and Guerrero, 1998: 56). This includes cases when people do not display worry and anxiety when one of their close friends or relatives has, for example, to undergo surgery. Instead, they display such emotions as felicity, hope, faith, and the like, to encourage the sick person (Rostomyan, 2020: 107).

The next stretch of discourse illustrates an example when one of the speakers, the leading person, feels an emotion on the inside, but demonstrates a completely different disposition to the state of affairs on the outside.

> Example: *"Fine, Shawanda. But the hard part's this afternoon."*

"Think they gonna believe me"

He thought no, but said yes.

(Gimenez, The Colour of Law, 2007: 428)

In this example, Shawanda is prosecuted being speculated to have killed a person. Yet, she is innocent. But as she is an Afro-American woman, she is not convinced that the jurors, the Judge and the audience would believe her. Nor is Scott. Nonetheless, he masks his doubt and convinces his client that they will believe her. The same holds true for leaders: they very often say things and do things even if they don't believe in the realization of them. As a result, the universe works in their benefit and profit.

Summarizing, we can state that in case we, as leaders and influencers, adhere to the aforementioned emotion expression management techniques appropriately, we will tune with the emotions of our collaborators and interactants; hence, we will stand a better chance of emotively positively influencing them and leading them towards a common goal.

Useful tips

To become a successful leader there are certain features:
1) **self-confidence,**
2) **decisiveness,**
3) **passion,**
4) **empathy,**
5) **goal-oriented,**
6) **dedication,**
7) **dream,**
8) **future-driven,**
9) **straightforwardness.**

There are also some useful tips to follow:
1) **communication skills,**
2) **listening skills,**
3) **interpersonal skills,**
4) **an eye for innovation,**
5) **continual learning,**
6) **resilience,**
7) **emotional intelligence.**

In case you follow the aforementioned steps and develop your skills in this direction by means of acquiring better communication, interpersonal and emotion management skills, you will eventually stand a better chance of becoming a successful leader, who is not afraid of innovation, dedication and failure and, moreover, sees an opportunity in each and every failure, as a winner is someone who never quit.

CONCLUSION

One of the main claims of the present book is that anyone can become a successful leader with special strategies.

Being a good leader requires certain skills, which can be mastered in successfully leading people towards a certain goal.

Nowadays, in terms of Neuroleadership and New Leadership, there is a distinct focus on the human resources, their special specific needs and requirements, feelings and emotions, and for this very reason a leader should not only focus on himself/herself or simply on the goal, but rather to take into consideration the needs of his/her people. This involves mastering diverse communication management and emotion management tools and techniques, which have been thoroughly discussed in this book.

It is our firm belief that by means of mastering efficient communication strategies and emotion management techniques and applying them in real-life situations, one can stand a great chance of becoming a good leader and succeeding in this life.

Our survey has also shown that emotion management and accurate emotional labour at workplace should be on the agenda of

both the leader and the followers in their interpersonal communicative interrelations to succeed.

In fact, it is also noteworthy that decision making processes are
also greatly affected by the positive and negative emotions of the
interactants, which we all should obviously be well-aware of.

Thus, in case we learn the communication management techniques and strategies described in this book, we will enhance our
emotional intelligence and consequently reach better results
both in our personal and professional lives.

To conclude with, we highly advise everybody to become open
communicators and learn more in leading others for the prosperity of the society.

Picture by Arman Sargsyan©

BIBLIOGRAPHY:

1. Andersen, Peter and Guerrero, Laura (1998). 'Principles of Communication and Emotion in Social Interaction.' In *Handbook of Communication and Emotion*, edited by Peter A. Andersen and Laura K. Guerrero. San Diego: Academic Press, pp. 49-96.

2. Arnold, M. B. (1960). *Emotion and Personality*. Volume I: *Psychological Aspects*. New York: Columbia University Press.

3. Austin, J.L. (1962). *How to Do Things with Words*. Oxford: Oxford University Press, 192 pages.

4. Backman, Carl. (1985). 'Identity, Self-presentation, and the Resolution of Moral Dilemmas: Toward a Social Psychological Theory of Moral Behaviour.' In *The Self and Social Life*, edited by B. L. Schlenker. New York: McGraw-Hill, pp. 261-289.

5. Bass, B.M. (1985). *Leadership and Performance beyond Expectations*. New York: Free Press.

6. Bolton, S. C. (2005). *Emotion Management in the Workplace*. Management, Work and Organisations, Palgrave.

7. Brannigan, Christopher and Humphries, David. (1969). 'I See What You Mean,' *New Scientist*, 42, pp. 406-408.

8. Bradberry, Travis & Greaves, Jean (2016). *Emotionale Intelligenz 2.0: erhöhen Sie Ihre Sozialkompetenz und verbessern Sie Ihre Kommunikation*. München: mvg Verlag.

9. Brown, R. (2009). *Public Relations and the Social Web: How to Use Social Media and Web 2.0 in Comunications*. London: Kogan Page.

10. Bühler, Karl (1999). *Sprachtheorie. Die Darstellungsfunktion der Sprache*. Mit einem Geleitw. von Friedrich Kainz. - 3. Aufl. - Stuttgart: G. Fischer. - XXXIV, 434 S. (UTB für Wissenschaft; 1159), here: pp. 24-33.

11. Buller, David and Burgoon, Judee (1998). 'Emotional Expression in the Deception Process.' In *Handbook of Communication and Emotion*, edited by Peter A. Andersen and Laura K. Guerrero. San Diego, CA: Academic Press, pp. 381-402.

12. Burgoon, Judee (1993). 'Interpersonal Expectations, Expectancy Violations, and Emotional Communication,' *Journal of Language and Social Psychology*, 12, pp. 30-48.

13. Buzarov, V. V. (1998). *Essentials of Conversational English Syntax*. Moscow: Crone-press.

14. Callahan, J. L. (2000). 'Emotion management and organizational functions: A case study of patterns in a not-for-profit organization'. *Human Resource Development Quarterly*, Volume 11, 3. pp. 245-267.

15. Camras, Linda (1982). 'Socialization of Affect Communication.' In *The Socialization of Emotions*, edited by M. Lewis and C. Saari. New York: Plenum Press, pp. 141-160.

16. Carnegie, Dale (1982). *How to Win Friends and Influence People*. New York, London, Toronto, Sydney: Pocket Books.

17. Castells, M. (2007). Communication, Power and Counter-power in the Network Society. *International Journal of Communication* 1.

18. Clore G., Ortony A. (2000). *Cognition in Emotion: Always, Sometimes, or Never?* Series in affective science. *Cognitive Neuroscience of Emotion.* R. Lane and L. Nadel (Eds.) NY: Oxford University Press, pp. 24–61.

19. Coleman, J. S. (1990). *Foundations on Social Theory.* Massachussetts: The Belknap Press and Harward University Press.

20. Damasio, A. (1994). *Descartes' Error: Emotion, Reason, and the Human Brain.* New York: G.P. Putnam's Sons.

21. Damasio, A. (1999). *The Feeling of what Happens: Body and Emotion in the Making of Consciousness.* New York: Harcourt Brace and Co.

22. Dennett, D. (1989). *The Neurobiology of Memory: Concepts, Findings, Trends.* New York: Oxford University Press.

23. Dennett, D. *Consciousness Explained.* New York: Little Brown, 1991.

24. De Sousa, R. (1987). *The Rationality of Emotion.* Cambridge MA: MIT Press.

25. Deutsch, M. (1958). "The Effects of Motivational Orientation upon Trust and Suspicion", *Human Relations*, vol. 13 Sage Publications, pp. 123-139.

26. Dijk, Teun A. van, and Kintsch W. (1977a). *Cognitive Psychology and Discourse*. In: W.U. Dressier, ed. Current trends in text linguistics. Berlin, New York: de Gruyter.

27. Dijk, Teun A. van. (1977b). *Text and Context. Explorations in the semantics and pragmatics of discourse*. London: Longmans.

28. Ekman, Paul (1979). *About Brows: Emotional and Conversational Signals*. In M. von Cranach, K. Foppa, W. Lepenies, D. Ploog (Eds), *Human Ethology*: Claims and Limits of a New Discipline: Contributions to the Colloquium, Cambridge: Cambridge University Press, pp. 169-248.

29. Ekman, Paul (2004). *Emotions Revealed: Recognizing Faces and Feelings to Improve Communication*. New York: Henry Holt and Company.

30. Ekman, Paul and Friesen, Wallace (1975). *Unmasking the Face: A Guide to Recognizing Emotions from Facial Clues*. Englewood Cliffs, NJ: Prentice-Hall.

31. Ekman, Paul, Friesen, Wallace and Ellsworth, Phoebe (1972). *Emotion in the Human Face: Guidelines for Research and an Integration of Findings*. New York: Pergamon Press.

32. Engwall, L., Kipping, M. and Üsdiken, B. (2016). *Defining Management: Business Schools, Consultants, Media*. New York and London: Routledge, Taylor & Francis Group.

33. Fineman, St. (Ed.) (2008). *The Emotional Organization: Passions and Power*. Blackwell: Malden.

34. Fineman, St. (Ed.) (2000). *Emotion in Organizations*. Sage: London.

35. Frager, R., & Fadiman, J. (2006). *Personality and Personal Growth*. Saint-Petersbourg: Prime-Evroznak.

36. Gimenez, Mark (2007). *The Colour of Law*. London: Sphere.

37. Goldie, P. (2000). *The Emotions: A Philosophical Exploration*. New York, Oxford: Oxford University Press.

38. Goleman, D. (1995). *Emotional Intelligence*. New York, Toronto, London, Sydney, Auckland: Bantam Books.

39. Graves, R.H. (1934). *The Triumph of an Idea: The Story of Henry Ford*. New York: Country Life Press.

40. Grice, H.P. (1969). *Utterer's Meaning and Intentions*. Philosophical Review, New York: Academic Press.

41. Grice, H.P. (1975). *Logic and Conversation*. In P. Cole & J. Morgan (Eds). Syntax and semantics, Vol. 3, New York: Academic Press.

42. Griffiths, P.E. (1997). *What Emotions Really Are*. London, Chicago: Chicago University Press.

43. Hartley, P. (1993). *Interpersonal Communication*. London: Routledge.

44. Heritage, J. (2005). *Cognition in Discourse*. Conversation and Cognition. H.te Moulder et al. Eds., Cambridge: Cambridge University Press.

45. Hochschild, A. R. (1983). *The Managed Heart: Commercialization of human feeling*. Berkeley: University of California Press.

46. Hochschild, A. R. (1990). *Research Agendas in the Sociology of Emotions.* SUNY series in the sociology of emotions. Albany, NY, US: State University of New York. pp. 117-142.

47. Hsieh, T. (2010). *Delivering Happiness: A Path to Profits, Passion, and Purpose.* New York, Boston: Business Plus Press.

48. Hutton, Chris (2009). *Language, Meaning and the Law.* Edinburgh: Edinburgh University Press.

49. James, W. (1890). *The Principles of Psychology.* Classics in the History of Psychology. An internet resource developed by Christopher D. Green of York University. Toronto, Ontario.

50. Kenning, P., Plassmann, H. (2005) *NeuroEconomics: an Overview from an Economic Perspective.* Brain Res Bull; 67:343–354.

51. Knapp, Mark and Comadena, Mark (1979). 'Telling It Like It Isn't: A Review of Theory and Research on Deceptive Communications,' *Human Communication Research*, 5, pp. 270-285.

52. Knowles, E., & Sibicky, M. (1990). Continuity and diversity in the stream of selves: Metaphorical resolutions of William Jame's one-in-many-selves paradox. *Personality and Social Psychology Bulletin*, 76(4), 676-687.

53. Lafferty, Christina L.; Alford, Kenneth L. (June 22, 2010). "NeuroLeadership: sustaining research relevance into the 21st century". *SAM Advanced Management Journal.* Retrieved March 30, 2012.

54. Lakoff, D. & Lu, F. (1989). Transpersonal psychology research review. Topic: Computerized databases, specialized collections. *Journal of Transpersonal Psychology*, 21(2), 211-223.

55. Levinson, S.C., (1983). *Pragmalinguistics*. Cambridge, UK: Cambridge University Press.

56. Lively, K. J. (2000). 'Reciprocal Emotion Management: Working Together to Maintain Stratification in Private Law Firms'. *Work and Occupations*, 27. pp. 32 – 63.

57. Murphy, G. & Ballou, R. (Eds.) (1960). *William James on Psychical research*. New York: Viking Press.

58. Malatesta, Carol and Izard, Carroll (1984). 'Conceptualizing Emotional Development in Adults.' In *Emotion in Adult Development*, edited by Carol Zander Malatesta and Carroll Ellis Izard. Beverly Hills: Sage Publications, pp. 13-21.

59. Malinowski, B. (1923). The Problem of Meaning in Primitive Languages. In *The Meaning of Meaning: A Study of Influence of Language Upon Thought and of the Science of Symbolism*. C. K. Ogden and I. A. Richards. New York: Harcourt, Brace and World, pp. 296-336.

60. Matsumoto, David (1991). 'Cultural Influences on Facial Expressions on Emotion,' *Southern Communication Journal: Patterns and Functions of Nonverbal Communication*, 56, pp. 128-137.

61. McTaggart, John Ellis (1927). *The Nature of Existence*. Vol. 2. Cambridge: Cambridge University Press.

62. Murray, E.J. (1964). *Motivation and Emotion*. New Jersey: Prentice-Hall, Inc.

63. Neale, M.A., Bazerman, M.H. (1994) *Negotiating* Rationality. *Journal of Business and Economics*, NY: Simon and Schuster, 196 p.

64. Nussbaum, M. (2001). *Upheavals of Thought: The Intelligence of Emotions*. Cambridge: Cambridge University Press, 766 p.

65. Ochsner, K.N., Gross, J. J. (2005). 'The Cognitive Control of Emotion'. *Trends in Cognitive Sciences*, Vol.9, No.5. Amsterdam: Elsevier Ltd, pp. 242-249.

66. O'Hair, Dan and Cody, Michael (1994). 'Deception.' In *The Dark Side of Interpersonal Communication*, edited by William R. Cupach and Brian H. Spitzberg. Hillsdale, NJ: Lawrence Erlbaum, pp. 181-213.

67. Paronyan, Sh., Rostomyan, A. (2011a). On the Interrelation between Cognitive and Emotional Minds in Speech. Armenian Folia Anglistika, *International Journal of English Studies*, 1-2(8), Yerevan: Lusakn Publishers, pp 26-33.

68. Paronyan, Sh., Rostomyan, A. (2011b). The Pragmatic Impact of Background Emotional Memory on Interpersonal Relations. Armenian Folia Anglistika, *International Journal of English Studies*, 2(9), Yerevan: Lezvakan Horizon, pp. 7-14.

69. Putman R. D. (2000). *Bowling Alone: The Collapse and Revival of American Community*. New York: Harper Collins.

70. Quandt, Throsten (2012). 'What's left of trust in a network society? An evolutionary model and critical discussion of trust and societal communication'. In: Peter Golding, Helena Sousa, Liesbet van Zoonen (Eds.) *European Journal of Communication*, volume 27 (1), UK: Sage Publications Ltd., pp. 7-21.

71. Rick, S. and Loewenstein, G. (2008). *Handbook of Emotions*, Third Edition, edited by Michael Lewis, Jeannette M. Haviland-Jones, and Lisa Feldman Barrett. US: The Guilford Press, pp. 138–156.

72. Rock, D. (2013). *Handbook of NeuroLeadership*. New York: CreateSpace Independent Publishing Platform.

73. Rock, D. (2007). *Quiet Leadership: Six Steps to Transforming Performance at Work*. New York: HarperBusiness

74. Rostomyan, Anna (2009). *Means of Expressing Emotive Emphasis in Conversational English*. Foreign Languages in Armenia, N10, Yerevan: YSU Press.

75. Rostomyan, Anna (2010). Emotions in Linguistic Behaviour. Armenian Folia Anglistika. *International Journal of English Studies*, 1-2(7). Yerevan: Lusakn Publishers, pp. 102-109.

76. Rostomyan, Anna (2012). *The Vitality of Emotional Background Knowledge in Court*, Polemos, 6(2), De Grutyer, pp. 281-292.

77. Rostomyan, Anna (2013a) Management Techniques of Emotions in Communicative Conflict Reduction, in part 3: Communication and Management, *Communication: Breakdowns and*

Breakthroughs, Probing the Boundaries, eds. Anabel Ternès, Inter-disciplinary Press, UK: Oxford, pp.141-151.

78. Rostomyan, Anna (2013b). *Huyzeri khoskayin ev voch khoskayin drsevorumnere vorpes lezvachanachoghakan qnnutyan ararka (angleren nyuti himan vra)/* A Linguo-cognitive Analysis on the Verbal and Non-verbal Expressions of Emotions (on the material of English fiction and films), dissertation, 160 pages, summary 27 pages, Yerevan, Armenia.

79. Rostomyan, A. and Sukiasyan, M. (2015). *"The Importance of Emotional Intelligence in Neuroleadership"*, Finance & Economics Journal, proceedings of the conference, Frankfurt am Main, Germany.

80. Rostomyan, Anna (2015). *"The Impact of Emotions in Decision making Processes in the Field of Neuroeconomics"*, Volume 6, Number 7, Academic Star Publishing Company, New York, USA, pp. 1268-1277.

81. Rostomyan, Anna, and Rostomyan, Armen (2018). Emotional Intelligence and Leadership, *Journal of Managerial Studies and Research*, 6(8), pp. 34-41.

82. Rostomyan, Anna (2020). *Business Communication Management: The Key to Emotional Intelliegnce*. Tredition: Hamburg.

83. Schulz von Thun, F., Ruppel, J. & Stratmann, R. (Hrsg.) (2003). *Miteinander reden: Kommunikation für Führungskräfte*. Reinbek: Rowohlt.

84. Schulz von Thun, F. (2004). *Klarkommen mit sich selbst und anderen: Kommunikation und soziale Kompetenz: Reden, Aufsätze, Dialoge*. Reinbek: Rowohlt.

85. Searle, J.R. (1969). *Speech Acts: An Essay in The Philosophy of Language*. Cambridge, UK: Cambridge University Press.

86. Searle, J.R. (1975). *Indirect Speech Acts*. In P. Cole & J. Morgan (Eds). Syntax and Semantics, Vol. 3, New York: Academic Press.

87. Sloan, M. M. (2012). 'Unfair Treatment in the Workplace and Worker Well-Being: The Role of Coworker Support in a Service Work Environment'. *Work and Occupation*, 39, pp. 3-34.

88. Solomon, R. C. (1980). *Emotions and Choice. Explaining Emotions*, Amélie Rorty (Ed.). Los Angeles: University of California Press.

89. Solomon, R. C. (1993). *The Passions: Emotions and the Meaning of Life*. Indianapolis, IN: Hackett Pub Co.

90. Ternès, A. & Rostomyan, A., (2011b). *Emotion Management in Business Ethics*. Living Responsibly Reflecting on the Ethical Issues of Everyday Life. Proceedings of the 2nd global conference on Managerial Studies organized by Inter-disciplianry.net. Prague.

91. Ternès, Anabel, Rostomyan, Anna, Gursch, Francesca, and Gursch, Giulia (2014). *"Levers of Personal Branding to Optimize Success"*, Volume 5, Number 1, Academic Star Publishing Company, USA, New York, pp. 86-94.

92. Verschueren, Jef (1999). *Understanding Pragmatics*. Amsterdam: Hodder Education Publishers.

93. Watzlawick, P., Beavin, J.H., Jackson, D. D. (1969). *Menschliche Kommunikation – Formen, Störungen, Paradoxien*. Bern: Huber.

94. Williams, M. (2007). Building Genuine Trust through Interpersonal Emotion Management: A Threat Regulation Model of Trust and Collaboration across Boundaries. *The Academy of Management Review Archive*. Vol. 2, No. 2. pp. 595 – 621.

95. Yule, G. (1996). *Pragmalinguistics*, Oxford Introductions to Language Study, series editor H. G. Widdowson. Oxford, New York: Oxford University Press.

FSC
www.fsc.org
MIX
Papier | Fördert
gute Waldnutzung
FSC® C083411

Zeitfracht Medien GmbH
Ferdinand-Jühlke-Straße 7
99095 Erfurt, Deutschland
produktsicherheit@kolibri360.de